10.⁰⁰

MY FIRST JOKES AND RIDDLES

How Do You Raise a Rhino?

by Judy Ziegler

GALLERY BOOKS
An Imprint of W. H. Smith Publishers Inc.
112 Madison Avenue
New York City 10016

An RGA Book

Where does a nine-foot rabbit sleep?

Anywhere it wants.

What time is it when an elephant sits in your lawn chair?

Time to get a new lawn chair.

What kind of animal can jump higher than a skyscraper?

All kinds. Skyscrapers can't jump!

5

Where do bees wait for rides?

At the buzz stop.

Why did the rabbit have a big hanky?

For crying out loud.

Should you eat pie on an empty stomach?

No. Eat it on a plate.

Why is a river rich?

It has two banks.

How do you make a banana split?

Cut it in half.

It takes 16 sheep to make a sweater.

How do you catch a squirrel?

Act like a nut.

What do kangaroos wear?

Jump suits.

What's gray, has whiskers, and rolls?

A mouse on a skateboard.

What's black and white and black and white and black and white?

A penguin rolling down a hill.

19

Why did the cat play the trumpet to her pancakes?

She was blowing her stack.

What flies, stings, and is hard to hear?

A mumble bee.

I had to get up in the middle of the night to answer the phone in my nightie.

Why did the hippo sit on his birthday cake?

He wanted to make a big impression.

What's the difference between a doughnut
and a warthog?

You can't dunk a warthog in your milk.

How did the skunk keep from smelling?

He held his nose.

Why did the raccoon put wheels on her rocking chair?

She wanted to rock 'n' roll.

Why was the gorilla surprised when bananas grew out of his ears?

He had planted watermelons.

What do you do with a bad pig?

Ham cuff him!

How many chickens can you put in an empty box?

One. Then the box isn't empty.